Estimating Your Money Gap

Providing for Retirement

Teresa M. O'Brien

Disclaimer

While helpful hints are provided throughout the book for completing the tables, they are in no way to be considered a substitute for legal and financial counsel. Please check with all the members of your professional team for the latest legal requirements and processes. O'Brien Consulting Group, LLC., assumes no responsibility for legal or financial processes.

ISBN: 978-1-7379432-6-6

First printing, 2022

O'Brien Consulting Group, LLC
Midland, MI 48640

Books on Organizing Personal Financial Information by the Author

Now What Do I Do? – Settling Your Spouses' Estate – Organizing and Simplifying the Process

Business and Personal Information Summary – For the Single Small Business Owner

What's My Potential Exposure to Estate Taxes? – Summarizing Data Your Accountant Needs to Estimate Your Estate Taxes

Our Money Summary – Summary of Our Family's Finances

My Money Summary – Summary of My Personal Finances

The Estate Settler's Organizer – For Settling an Unmarried Friend or Family Member's Estate

Estimating Your Money Gap – Providing for Retirement

All are available on www.Amazon.com

Table of Contents

INTRODUCTION

Why I Did This Exercise for Myself:

Financial advisors can estimate what any current stock, bond, cash, and CD portfolio will likely grow to in the next ten-plus years. Therefore, my advisor could give me a fairly good idea of what my nest egg would grow to, based on the current allocation of my money, and assuming no money was added to or taken out of the funds.

But to really address my retirement situation he also needed to know how much income and expenses I had and would likely have going forward. This would help determine how much additional savings I could add to my nest egg and when I might need to withdraw from it.

In the past, my advisor had used a ballpark estimate of what my current income and expenses were without a breakdown of expenses into categories. That was fine when I was far from retirement. But once retirement loomed as a reality, a generic answer didn't feel sufficient.

So, I did the exercise that I will be discussing in this book. I looked at my income and expenses for the current year, five years out and ten years out. I pulled together the information at a detailed enough level that I could see where I was spending my money in various categories.

One of the most important parts of the exercise was to know when, or if, my annual expenses would exceed my annual income. Once that happened, I would need to tap into my savings to pay some or all of my expenses.

Therefore, I focused on whether I was going to have a surplus of funds in each of the three years I analyzed. As long as my income was exceeding my outgo, I could target some or all of those yearly excess funds into my savings and investing, which would continue to grow my reserve funds.

I looked at the trend over those three time periods to see if there was a decrease in the surplus of funds that I had each year. If the surplus was increasing, I figured that increased the likelihood that my funds would last. If the amount of excess funds was decreasing, that meant I might either need to have a larger surplus of funds or else find ways to cut back on my spending.

This exercise led me to better understand:

- How much I would likely add to my retirement reserves in the next 10 years
- When I would start using my reserves to pay for some of my expenses
- How much I would need to draw down each year once I started using my reserve funds.

This led me to ask: how can I reduce my expenses or increase my income in order to delay drawing on my savings for as long as possible and still live the life I love?

By breaking my spending into several areas, it was easier to see where expenses were increasing the fastest and, therefore, where I should focus my initial attention. This way I wasn't being unnecessarily strict or wildly optimistic about how much I needed to save or where to make adjustments.

I used this exercise not only to assess my retirement situation but also to revise my annuity portfolio. Over the years I had acquired several annuities. Looking at them, in light of the exercise I describe in this book, my advisor and I agreed that not all of them were right for my situation. As a result, we made some changes. Now my assets are better aligned to meet my future needs.

This exercise has given me great peace of mind. Every couple of years I update the information on my income and expenses, which allows me to make sure that I am still on track.

Why I Wrote This Book:

I created this book to show you how you can do the same exercise. Since it took me a couple of times using the information before I settled on the format that is in this book, I thought I would share my tables to shorten your process of finding what works best for you. Use the tables in this book as is or modify them to fit your needs.

This booklet is designed to help you identify:

1. All your current sources and amounts in your nest egg
2. Your current income
3. Your current expenses
4. Major life changes you see for you and your family over the next five to ten years
5. Where and when these life changes will affect your income and expenses and by how much

This information can be used by your financial advisor to adjust for inflation in projecting your financial information to determine how likely you are to achieve your retirement dream.

CALCULATING A MONEY GAP

How I Projected My Money Gap:

First, I summarized my current income. Then, I determined my future income – including pension and Social Security – using the pension calculator from my company and Social Security's annual estimate, to determine how much money I was likely to receive each year.

My pension is a fixed amount once I started it, but the Social Security amount will increase over time, based on a cost-of-living adjustment (COLA) that the federal government decides each year. The average annual COLA has been 1.7% annually. This number varies over time with a wide range of annual increases. For example, for 2022 the COLA is 5.9%.

Next, I looked at my expenses. I first determined how much I was currently spending and where. Then I projected forward.

For those areas that I thought would increase with the rate of inflation (utilities, car maintenance, household supplies, etc.), I simply used the historical rate of inflation of the Consumer Price Index (CPI) for the last 10 years (currently 2.5%). Since medical expenses had a compounded average growth rate of 5%, I used that number. For the fixed-rate mortgage, I kept the number constant until I had it paid off.

Then I looked at my net worth to determine how much stocks, bonds, and cash I had saved for my reserve funds to draw on in the future. I used a conservative 5%/year growth for my stock and bond combined portfolio. I used the interest rates I was getting on cash and CDs as the rate going forward for those funds.

Then I applied these estimates of spending increases. I liked doing these calculations, but you can get your advisor to run them for you.

An Example for Filling in the Tables:

A single person is 55 years old. Her current salary is $5,000 a month. Her monthly $800 mortgage will be paid off in three years. Her food, clothing, entertainment, and home repairs are $1,500 per month, her car payment is $400 per month, and her income and property taxes are $750 per month. House, medical, and car insurance together are $1,150 per month. She has out-of-pocket medical expenses of $80 per month and she donates $50 per month to charity. This leaves her $270 per month to invest in savings. She has not started her pension or Social Security.

So, her income and expenses for the current year look like this:

Table 1 – Current Income and Expenses Summary

ITEM	Year 2022
ANNUAL INCOME	
Paycheck	**$60,000**
Pension	**0**
TOTAL INCOME	**$60,000**
ANNUAL EXPENSES	
Housing	**$9,600**
Transportation	**$4,800**
Taxes	**$9,000**
Insurance	**$13,800**
Daily living, Home repairs	**$18,000**
Medical	**$960**
Charity	**$600**
Savings	**$3,240**
TOTAL EXPENSES	**$60,000**

In five years, when she is 60 years old, both her car and house will be paid off. Her salary will be $66,000 annually. Her combined insurance will be $1,300 per month and her taxes will be $900 per month. Her daily living expenses and home repairs will be $1,700 monthly, her out-of-pocket medical expenses will be $100 monthly, and her charity contributions will be $75 monthly. This will leave her with a monthly savings of $1,425.

Table 2 – Current and Five-Year Estimated Income and Expenses Summary

ITEM	Year 2022	Year 2027
ANNUAL INCOME		
Paycheck	$60,000	$66,000
Pension		
TOTAL INCOME	$60,000	$66,000
ANNUAL EXPENSES		
Housing	$9,600	$0
Transportation	$4,800	$0
Taxes	$9,000	$10,800
Insurance	$13,800	$15,600
Daily living, Home repairs	$18,000	$20,400
Medical	$960	$1,200
Charity	$600	$900
Savings	$3,240	$17,100
TOTAL EXPENSES	$60,000	$66,000

Ten years from now, at age 65, she will purchase a new car. Her car payment will be $750 per month. Her salary will be $69,000. Her insurance costs will be $1,470 per month, daily living and house repairs will be $1,925 per month. Her out-of-pocket medical expenses are estimated to be $130 per month, her charity contributions will be $85 per month. Her savings will be $370 per month and her taxes will be $1,020 per month.

Table 3 – Current, 5-Year, and 10-Year Estimated Income and Expenses Summary

ITEM	Year 2022	Year 2027	Year 2032
ANNUAL INCOME			
Paycheck	$60,000	$66,000	$69,000
Pension			
TOTAL INCOME	$60,000	$66,000	$69,000
ANNUAL EXPENSES			
Housing	$9,600	$0	$0
Transportation	$4,800	$0	$9,000
Taxes	$9,000	$10,800	$12,240
Insurance	$13,800	$15,600	$17,640
Daily living, Home repairs	$18,000	$20,400	$23,100
Medical	$960	$1,200	$1,560
Charity	$600	$900	$1,020
Savings	$3,240	$17,100	$4,440
TOTAL EXPENSES	$60,000	$66,000	$69,000

YOUR MONEY GAP

How You Can Do the Same:

This analysis is especially useful for those who are nearing retirement. Having peace of mind is so much better than having a state of terror so great that you don't even want to think about retirement. You may also find that just doing this exercise gives you ideas on where you can save with little pain.

Knowing (1) what your income and expenses currently are and (2) how much your assets and liabilities are currently worth will make it easier to complete the exercises in this book. If you don't already know those details, you might find my previous books *My Money Summary* (if you are single) or *Our Money Summary* (if you are married) helpful.

Your data can be divided into three different time frames – your current year, five years out, and ten years out. For those who are farther than ten years away from retirement, you can do an estimate in the year you plan to retire.

The starting point is to look at where you are now. Determine what your income and expenses are today. Once you have your current year's expenses and income identified, estimate your income and expenses for the other two years you will use in your analysis.

Step 1 – In the last twelve months, how much income did you have?

Step 2 – How much did you spend last year? Break this down into several categories. Use these in Table 4 or modify categories to better reflect your needs.

Summarize your current income and expense information in Table 4.

Table 4 – Current Income and Expenses Summary

ITEM	Year 20____
ANNUAL INCOME	
Paycheck	
Pension	
Social Security	
TOTAL INCOME	
ANNUAL EXPENSES	
Housing	
Transportation	
Taxes	
Daily living, Home repairs	
Entertainment	
Medical	
Charity	
Savings	
TOTAL EXPENSES	

Step 3 – For your five-year analysis note any major events that will significantly change your income or expenses (get married, have children, buy a house, downsize to a smaller house, pay off a mortgage, start pension, etc.). How much will each of these changes impact your income and expenses? Use Table 5 to summarize this information.

Make sure to state whether the numbers that you have written for the future year are expressed in today's dollars or in the future year's dollars. This will help your financial advisor to complete the projection.

If you are still working, you can look back over your annual income for the last several years and calculate the rate of increase in annual income, to estimate how much your pay will increase in the future.

Table 5
What big changes do you see in your life in the next five years that will impact your income and expenses? When will each impact your finances? By how much?

Factor those changes from Table 5 into your future income or expenses in Table 6. For the rest of the items, your financial planner can estimate likely rates of increase in the various categories. This will then be the basis for your advisor to calculate the likelihood that your money will outlive you.

Table 6 – Current and Estimated Future Income and Expenses Summary

ITEM	Year 20____	Year 20____
ANNUAL INCOME		
Paycheck		
Pension		
Social Security		
TOTAL INCOME		
ANNUAL EXPENSES		
Housing		
Transportation		
Taxes		
Insurance		
Daily living, Home repairs		
Medical		
Charity		
Savings		
TOTAL EXPENSES		

Step 4 – Repeat the process in Step 3 for your tenth year. For your ten-year analysis note any major events that will significantly change your income or expenses (get married, have children, buy a house, downsize to a smaller house, pay off a mortgage, start pension, etc.). How much will each of these changes impact your income and expenses? Use Table 7 to summarize this information.

Make sure to state whether the numbers that you have written in the future year are expressed in today's dollars or in the future year's dollars. This will help your financial advisor to complete the projection. Fill in the resulting income and expenses in your last target year in Table 8.

Table 7
What big changes do you see in your life in the next ten years that will impact your income and expenses? When will each impact your finances? By how much?

Step 5 – Have your financial advisor enter your information from Tables 5 – 8 into their program so you can better see where you are heading. By taking even this much time to estimate information for your life situation, you and your advisor will feel more comfortable with the results.

Doing this exercise can perhaps make it easier for you to see the importance of cutting expenses and saving more for retirement if you aren't already saving enough.

I encourage you to make the easiest changes first to build momentum and to see that you can do this. Drop those expenses that no longer bring you joy.

Conclusion:

I hope this makes it easier for you to make any changes, as it did for me. And that your retirement becomes a reality with less suffering than you imagined. Working on creating the reality that you want with less stress and more joy – what a great contribution to your life and to the world!

Table 8 – Current and Estimated Future Income and Expenses Summary

ITEM	Year 20____	Year 20____	Year 20___
ANNUAL INCOME			
Paycheck			
Pension			
Social Security			
TOTAL INCOME			
ANNUAL EXPENSES			
Housing			
Transportation			
Insurance			
Daily living, Home repairs			
Medical			
Charity			
Savings			
TOTAL EXPENSES			

Key Takeaways

Use Table 9 to summarize your net worth and how much savings you have to cover any shortfall of funds. Most experts recommend drawing down not more than 4% of your savings each year in retirement.

To help you see how much 4% would be from each element of your retirement savings, I have included the Column Labelled "Financial Assets x 4%" in Table 9. To determine that number, multiply the amount of each of the assets in the top half of Table 9 by 0.04. For example, if you have $100,000 in brokerage accounts, 4% of that amount would be $100,000 x 0.04 = $4,000.

When you are working on increasing your savings, don't be discouraged at only being able to save a small amount at the beginning. As you start saving, you will see more opportunities to save. If it is only $100 after the first year, remember that is $100 more you saved than the previous year. Now you can start getting your money to work for you, not just you working for your money.

Table 9 – Net Worth

ITEM	VALUE	FINANCIAL ASSETS x 4%
House		--------------
Bank Accounts		
Brokerage Accounts		
Qualified Retirement Plans		
Insurance Surrender Value		
Annuity Surrender Value		
Other		
TOTAL ASSETS		--------------
4% of Financial Assets	--------------	
Mortgages		--------------
Student Loans		--------------
Car Loans		--------------
Notes Payables		--------------
Credit Card Balances		--------------
Other		--------------
TOTAL LIABILITIES		--------------
NET WORTH (ASSETS *MINUS* LIABILITIES)		--------------

(1) What are your key takeaways?

Look at the trends in your numbers in Table 8 and the amount of savings you have in Table 9. Are you saving enough for retirement? What area(s) deserve more of your attention over the next year or so?

(2) What one – three things will you do differently?

For each area, identify what you will do differently to see results change in those areas over the next several years.

___

(3) What are the key points you want to discuss with your financial advisor or others?

Talk to your advisor about these areas where you want to see change happen in your financial life. It's important for you and your advisor to be on the same page so your funds are in financial products consistent with your future needs.

Dated: _____

Other Financial Workbooks by Teresa

Situation	Solution	QR Code and URL to Amazon Book Page
Widow or widower settling their deceased spouse's estate	*Now What Do I Do?* *Settling Your Spouse's Estate – Organizing and Simplifying the Process*	https://qrs.ly/mxe03gh
Friend or loved one settling estate of a person who was single at time of death	*The Estate Settler's Organizer – For Settling an Unmarried Friend or Family Member's Estate*	https://qrs.ly/2ge03hu
Summary of financial and other key information of a married couple (with or without dependent children)	*Our Money Summary – Summary of Family's Finances*	https://qrs.ly/7de03h8
Summary of financial and other key information for an unmarried adult (including recent graduate, widow, divorced, and with or without children)	*My Money Summary – Summary of My Personal Finances*	https://qrs.ly/o6e03ic
Outlining your income, expenses, and savings now & in future, so your financial planner can estimate if you will have enough money for your retirement	*What's My Potential Exposure to Estate Taxes?* *Summarizing Data Your Accountant Needs to Estimate Your Estate Taxes*	https://qrs.ly/3qe03ho
Summarizing key personal and business information for a single, solo business owner, in case of emergency	*Business and Personal Information Summary - for the Single Small Business Owner*	https://qrs.ly/bge03i7

Your Opinion Is Important

It will help me improve this book and help other readers know what to expect.

If you have an Amazon account, you can scan the QR code below or use the URL to leave a review. *You may be requested to log in to your Amazon account to complete the review form.*

Let me know what you liked best, what was missing, if there was anything you would leave out, or anything else that's on your mind about the book.

Thanks!

https://qrs.ly/eze01pb

www.ingramcontent.com/pod-product-compliance
Lightning Source LLC
Chambersburg PA
CBHW071444210326
41597CB00020B/3937